Time Travel

poems by

Charlotte G. Morgan

Finishing Line Press
Georgetown, Kentucky

Time Travel

Copyright © 2020 by Charlotte G. Morgan
ISBN 978-1-64662-257-3 First Edition
All rights reserved under International and Pan-American Copyright Conventions. No part of this book may be reproduced in any manner whatsoever without written permission from the publisher, except in the case of brief quotations embodied in critical articles and reviews.

ACKNOWLEDGMENTS

"at the movies" was previously published in *The Hollins Critic*
"Tiny Tears" was published in *Lumina*
"Bivalve" and "Time Travel" were published in *Streetlight*
"Camille" "Gone Are the Days," and "Pain Assessment Scale" were published in *Artemis*
"Homemade," "Ubiquitous Presence," and "Almost Home" were juried for public presentation by New River Valley Voices.

Publisher: Leah Maines
Editor: Christen Kincaid
Cover Art: "Conundrum," collage by John Dure Morgan
Author Photo: Alex Herzog and Sasha Savenko
Cover Design: Elizabeth Maines McCleavy

Order online: www.finishinglinepress.com
also available on amazon.com

Author inquiries and mail orders:
Finishing Line Press
P. O. Box 1626
Georgetown, Kentucky 40324
U. S. A.

Table of Contents

I. FORMATIVE

at the movies 1
Bivalve 2
Excavating 3
Tiny Tears 4
Homemade 6
"Gone are the days…" 7
Que Pasa? 8

II. SCHISMS

Last Words 10
March 16, Six p.m. 11
Camille 12
Time Travel 13
C Words 15
Ubiquitous Presence 16
Voice 18
Alarmed 19
The Letter 20
Pain Assessment Scale 21
Names and Numbers: The Stockton Massacre 23
Almost Home 24

III. SETTLING

Skywriting 26
Growing Wild 27
Cast-Offs 28
Women, Bags 29
Continuity 31
Resurrection Lilies 32
I grow things 33
Greek Mythology 34

I. FORMATIVE

at the movies

Goetze's caramel
creams,
bull's-eye white
center—
perfect paired with chewy tan
taffy.

By myself
at the movies
I'd savor the whole pack
of sugary treats,
watch Scarlett and
Rhett, crave
romance, even loss,
like theirs.

Later, in the dark
balcony with my first forbidden
boyfriend, sticky mouth smeared
with kisses,
I grin: saucy, smug,
tasted.

Bivalve

Dull, grayish-white shell
shaped like my grandmother's locket,
I'm holding only part of you.
Beneath the ridged surface,
on the smooth underside,
I spot the shiny brown place
where life was once connected.

I remember the time my mother
took me and Toni White to Buckroe Beach,
how we giggled in the surf
listening to "Bye-Bye Love,"
paraded our fourteen-year-old bodies
in front of the lifeguard.
I met Clarence Strickland that summer.
Sunburned, we zig-zagged along
the shore at night
finding shells, making promises,
touching still-hot skin.

And the time at Nags Head
in the hurricane
when all the lights
on the island went out,
black as the bottom of the ocean.
Pressed against the headboard
I held my daughter
clutched to my milky breast
while my husband stayed up and watched
the storm.

I'm holding only half this shell;
the other part is missing,
washed away, disconnected,
leaving this remnant,
this relic, this barren vestige.

Excavating

In leggings, mittens, with crusty red noses
    me, my brothers, and the neighbor kids spent wintry afternoons
        digging with spoons to unearth this mysterious stone formation.

What was it? Some natural thing, created by Lord Jesus,
    or an alien object, split deep into the earth from outer space,
        or even a sealed coffin, a tomb, or a heavy box of treasure?

In school we'd learned about the mummies, gone to see the robbed grave
    at the museum, peeking deep into dark, wide eyes adjusting, silent
        when the blurred body came clear.

For years, my diary hidden from prying eyes, I told it secrets,
    buried them. Who might unearth it, find out about my forbidden
    boyfriend,
        our tiptoes quiet in the hallway, his furtive kisses down there…

What to do with buried things, before we die?
    We could attach them to wills, divisive codicils. Or give them to Goodwill.
        Or maybe, like retinas, donate them, for strangers to see, when we no
        longer can.

Or leave them hidden for curious grown children to find.
    In pitch dark I startle, can't breathe. Last night,
        the night before, digging through night terrors I wake, trembling.

Tiny Tears

1.
Eight, small—
"Like a doll," my mother says—
I pull back from the enormous
bearded red face.
"Tiny Tears," I whisper,
cringing, needing to climb down,
to escape white-gloved hands
holding me.
This real Santa Claus, enthroned
at Miller & Rhoads until Christmas Eve,
is bound to bring me what
I want.

Christmas morning
Tiny Tears sits under
our tree,
stiff arms outstretched,
a prickly brown wig
hugging her sculpted head.
I try to tear
away those curls, to make her
the soft hairless one I wanted.
When I offer a bottle
of water
she spurts
real tears.
But I never will be
her mother.

2.
My womanly 13-year-old
daughter demands,
"What do you want
for Christmas?
Tell me.
And *don't* say
      A happy day
again this year."

So now, this morning of Christ's birth,
I use a sharp knife
to make slits
in the leg of lamb,
shove garlic cloves into
the gaping wounds
while tears dampen
my cheeks.
I look down at my hands, greasy, bloody—at what I've chosen
for Christmas.

Homemade

1946 - 1956

She'd hammer a ten-penny nail
into the rounded end of a coconut,
always three holes. Milky
thin liquid would drip all day
into a glass, slow as sorghum.

After, she'd pound the brown hairy
skull, crack it open to the glaring white
meat. Piece by jagged piece
she'd shred it. Eggs, vanilla, flour
sugar, coconut milk—she'd beat

them all and pour thick batter into silvery tins.
While three layers baked she'd boil
seven-minute frosting into thick peaks, and I'd lick
the cakebowl until it shone, the milk
of coconut sweet on my tongue,

our tiny house exotic for that scented hour.
After Christmas dinner she'd present
this wonder of a cake, a shaggy white crown
on a cut-glass tiered stand, stiff
and grand, to slice into golden wedges,

my grandmother's sole gift to our crowded family.
Now I ponder: How did she, who never left
our city house, who sent my mother to shop
for weekly groceries, how did this country
woman learn to make this regal coconut cake?

"Gone are the days…"

Title derives from the song "Old Black Joe"

She came to the house every week, mostly
twice a week. Wire thin, tall, skin as dark as
a ripe avocado, she wore a maid's uniform, told me
how she once crossed the mountains on a mule.

She was "the ironing girl." This puzzled
me, as I was a girl and she was at least fifty,
maybe even one hundred. How could we both
be girls? Why did she wear white shoes like a baby's?

She rode the city bus to us. Besides ironing,
she'd hang out laundry, polish the silver,
scrub the kitchen floor, but nevertheless
she was always only "the ironing girl."

She called me Miss Char-let, but I was told
to call her Lillian. She taught my big brother,
Mr. Jimmy, how to smoke when he was twelve.
She sat with the family at my wedding, started

working for me when I had my second child.
"You and Mr. Jimmy had a lot better manners
when you was little." That was when my son
put a whoopee cushion in her chair.

She had to stop her day work. When she died, shrunken
to the size of her black porcelain doll, I put on
a white picture hat, with one dark red rose—
Lillian did admire style—and sang loud at her service.

"Que Pasa?"

I.
That muggy June day she walks
the three blocks to Grace Hospital,
leaving the two-year-old son
with Ruthie, a neighbor.
"You'll be a big brother today";
quick contractions tell her
the sister will come before dark.

Leaning swollen against the doorway,
trying not to pant, she waits
to leave the brick row house where she lives
in upstairs rooms with the boy
and his boy-father, a Navy cook
home from the sea
harboring dreams of his own café
one day. Pulling on
a ribbed muscle-T
the man walks her,
heavy on his arm,
to Grace Hospital to
bear the child.

Soon after that birth day
the sailor shoves off,
drowned in a sea of
bills and bitter words.
Sighing, she cooks the meals and
scrubs clean
the children's clothes,
waits on tables,
always waiting.

II.
Holiday Inn, refuge for wanderers, rises
where apartment rooms held afloat
the young woman's stifled laughs,
the husband's whispered plans.

Two blocks up, where the hospital once lived,
once cared for the sick and dying and birthing

those forty years ago, Chambaud House
now tends empty-eyed homeless
in its drab, echoing halls.

The big brother sleeps
in Heavenly Acres, checked out, not able
to face day after day his ever-carping mother.
"One of the funny ones"
boys pointed and jeered
on the bus that last day, on his way
to his shrink.

III.
The sister never visits his grave.
She walks five miles a day
listening to oldies on her Walkman,
pounding cinders,
planning what she'll have
for supper
tonight and the next years
of nights.

IV.
In Wisconsin a blind man can hunt.
He only has to have a sighted friend
aim the gun,
and he can shoot.

II. SCHISMS

Last Words

For Nancy, at 36

I lean in toward the whisper
of her wobbly voice, the only sound
in this dark room, but still so soft
as to be more like baby's breath
talk than words.

She's statue still, remote, waiting for her
seachange. All these months she's fought
this shift, but today she's going
nonetheless, whatever that means,
by herself.

I lean in toward her shallow breaths:
"It's not so bad." Wait. And again.
"It hurts so bad." Is that it? I can't
tell, can't ask *What did you say?*
I'll
never
know.

March 16, Six p.m.

Outside a restaurant named Rapture
I'm waiting in the twilight.
Two cellists are playing
classical tunes, thrumming strings
in the almost-spring air.
Shadowy chill chases
away sunlight, and I
start to shiver as the bench
cools beneath me.

Young mothers pushing
umbrollas scutter along,
their sandaled feet click-
clacking on uneven bricks.
Pizza and espresso aromas
waft in evening breeze.
Lights, like a crown, flash
on above me, the Paramont marquee.

Twenty-six years we're celebrating
tonight. Still, I'm waiting.
Down the mall a guitarist wails
"That's what I want."
Five forty-five we've decided; you hate
to be late. I look both ways:
I'll know your body before I glimpse
your face; no one walks as fast as you,
except me.

Six fifteen. The cellists have gone.
Lights dance around the showcase
shouting: Indigo Girls! Eight o'clock!
Sold out!
Where are you?
I'm waiting.

Camille

I remember my daughter astride a headstone
calling, "Take one of me, too," as
I snapped the facts I'd read about,
haunted by this hillside
Camille washed clean.
Rodger, Rebecca, Mitchell C., James and Annie—
all Huffmans lost, memorialized,
graven in gray stone.

Another sixteen rest, eternally recovering
from the blows of Paleolithic
rock and mud,
air full of bark and grass
too thick with rain to breathe.
Five hours, thirty-seven inches, one hundred twenty
dead.
Now the Huffman family reunion here, on this green hill,
as gently grazing cows guard
above them.

Audrey Zirkle, barely sixteen,
home early from band practice,
hung all night in a tree, calling "Hold on"
to her sister. She wasn't there
the next morning.
Found days later by her Fancy Dress date,
shiny skin almost overlooked, the color
of the sand that buried her.
She was naked to the waist, preserved
like one of those ship's ladies recovered
after centuries, head arching upward, on the floor
of the sea.
Red gladiolus rise up from her urns,
the color of her corsage the night she
danced and danced.

Time Travel

I used to take
the train
everywhere.

Santa's Helpers they called
us, high school girls in
red jumpers giving out candy,
leading carols, charming children
on the Santa Train to
Ashland to pick up
the Snow Queen
and her phony elf.

Once, spring break, money spent,
not a nickel in my change
purse, I sat up all
night, from Homestead to
Richmond, shivering, hungry.

"It's not nice to say
shut up, man," my boy
said on the way to Fort
Lauderdale, where we
picked limes in the back
yard and saw orchids, waves of orchids,
inside a restaurant.

The Silver Meteor pushed
three boys off the
trestle tracks. I waited,
watched divers pull
two motorcycles out of
the river, saw a mother
scream.

Those paper cone
cups for water,
the dining car's shining
metal teapots, the rough-textured
surface of the seats—

I used to take
the train
everywhere.

C Words

Cyst has a soft sound,
she's a silky sister
unlike that other hard
crafty cackling C word.

Soft, as in cygnet,
cymbal and ceasefire,
a gentle *s* sound, soothing
to the ear when the surgeon
says it.

That other bad boy,
that harsh *c* sound
like can't and controlling
and cunt, he's a coward,
a cowboy, a real cocksucker
of a word.

Hold on a sec, could cyst
be colluding with that coarse C cousin,
does it have a soupçon of cemetery in it?
Cyst—wait, no, now I hear it, that slippery,
scissory hiss, like cyanide.

Ubiquitous Presence

I only meant to glance,
Sergeant Locklear,
a voyeur passing by your gung-ho group,
glancing never glaring
at the soldiers breaking down their sharp displays,
the Global Presence packing their containers,
recruits rolling up the Ryder ramp next to
borders of marching pansies and tulips and flox.

Militant muscles bulge in
tan T-shirts, camouflage pants,
some with green berets, others with camo ball caps or
only bristly nearly-shaven heads.
Pacifist objector, that's me,
Sergeant Locklear:
English professor colliding head-on with Army recruiter.

I didn't mean to hassle you,
Sergeant Locklear,
when you quick-stepped over and introduced yourself
blunt firm hand extended.
I meant to walk on by, only peek.
Neat, everything folded up, sealed in, squared off neat.
Black display screens rolled into tubes, rubber containers clipped,
          strapped, stored for the next showcase.

"These guys are the elite of the elite,"
you offer, Sergeant Locklear:
"Army Special Forces, all with better than 1200 on their college boards.
They speak two languages, mostly serve in South America."
"You don't say," I can only force my answer.
Like Army ants the soldiers keep on packing.
Team de la Team.

Please don't think me rude,
Sergeant Locklear,
when I say goodbye and hurry on my way.
My baby brother was drafted in your Army,
a medic in Viet Nam, never cream de la anything
after that.
My older brother flew to Ton Se Nut,

a second Lewie in the US Air Force.
He wore stars at VMI, was Number One in his class of engineers.
When he came home he sealed his car and pumped in fumes,
empty beer bottles his final comrades in arms.

So I hope you don't suspect,
Sergeant Locklear,
that I wish I'd only glanced and passed you by.

Voice

Like a lightning bolt
the airplane strikes the first tower.

Driving along the interstate,
uncertain I'd heard correctly,
I make my hesitant hand turn
the dark volume dial.

Crossing Longdale Bridge, as I
do every day on my way
to school, I hear this distant
voice, an angel of death,
intone the tragedy of
my ordinary fall day.

Alarmed

Alarmed, I felt a crushing pain today,
a clamor and commotion in my head.
I did not think I'd live past dawn this way.

The noise became those words I'd heard you say
when you woke me in the night, above my bed;
off guard, I felt a crushing pain today.

You swore that you would never go astray,
although at first I'd put you off, with dread.
I did not think I'd ever wake this way.

The morning light pierced in with chilling grey
like icy knives sharp as a cruel lead;
unhinged, I felt a crushing pain today.

"You'll forget me"—did you utter that cliché?
Like a letter bomb it exploded my last thread
of calm; I could not breathe at all this way.

No Romeo, you left the coward's way;
and now, I try to hate you but instead,
alarmed, I feel this crushing pain today:
I do not think I'll live past dawn this way.

The Letter

That curled capital C—
cramped, disconnected letters forming
my name, my home address, in blue
ballpoint—who would write me from Montana?—
a pre-stamped envelope, some junk mail
look-alike
from Inmate # 5492063.

I know who that is.

That blink between one moment and the next, my missing son
isn't missing any more.
This letter on my dining room table, benign
as the others, stings like scraped knees.
He's been gone two years.
       "Say good-bye, Mother. This is good-bye,"
in that flat across-the-wires voice
that wasn't his
at all.

And now this envelope, this object
riveting my vision:
      It's from Gregg.

I can't touch it.
I have to touch it.

I pick it up, like any piece of paper—
      not hot, not cold,
only unresponsive paper.

Should I conjure some ceremony?
Just squiggles on an envelope,
and I can't move.
His letter, in my hands, for me
to open.

Pain Assessment Scale

Cold logic only a medical
institution could impose:

On a scale of one to ten, how much
pain do you feel?

We cruise through life at level one, even
sleeping, drunk on pot, during orgasm.

What would be a three?
The first contraction. Name a five.

The moment of reality: He died on impact.
Or a week later, alone after the casseroles:

which of those pains warrants a six?
Maybe both are only fives.

Eva Kor, in Auschwitz:
"We didn't get to say goodbye."

That must be a—let's see—a seven.
After all, she got to keep her hair.

Those parents of twins given Heparin:
Was it an eight when the first one died?

But save that eight, give it a seven,
Save eight for the girl dying, too.

But what number suits both arms cut off,
left bleeding but alive?

Or "I lived: the intruder killed my wife, burned
my house, my two daughters suffocated in the fire"?

That woman who died on the floor
of the ER—she could've been a ten.

I've got it: Jumping from the East Tower,
last gasp, screaming into burning air and ash:

no way down, no way out, no more time—
That instant: total pain. That's it, a ten.

I envision the jumping man, the dying woman, screaming,
as if some doctor somewhere could hear:

"Ten!"

Names and Numbers: Stockton School Massacre

January 17, 1989

Raphanar Or, Ram Chun, Thuy Tran, Sokhem An, Oeun Lim—
names buried on page five,
faceless figures in a bloody red schoolyard.
Morning and evening papers, an old mugshot
of Patrick Purdy, 24, makes the front page.

Six o'clock telly reports him sweeping his AK-47
deadly calm, TV come to life
for screaming children
scattered
like jacks
on the playground.
"Satan" on his chest, cold fury
in his head, he stalks
the ti-ti gooks
who made it
to the Promised Land.

School photos of the children
flash like gunfire
across the bright screen,
a dizzying blur
of shining black hair, shy smiles, starched white collars.

My daughter, listening, holds up
two five-year-old fingers:
"Did the bad man kill this many, Mommy?"
I burst open a fist full in reply:
"No, this many."
"Will he hurt me?"
"No, he can't." Hurt you.

Yesterday's figures, today's information,
Replenished at six and eleven
by a fresh new offering
of names and numbers.
They bind me to the screen,
become welded in my brain,
this one event immeasurable,
like no other.

Almost Home

I've pulled off the highway
to find a bite to eat:
home in three hours, at the outside.

The hostess can't be a day over sixteen.
The burger is dry, inedible, my coffee old.
The waitress can't count change.

I say to the self-tagged manager
"The service was awful," and
he smiles.

It's gotten dark out and the lot
reminds me of film noir, only
lonelier, danker.

Where are the cars?

I can't find my keys, can't feel them
in my purse, in my pockets.
The cell phone's on the console: I can see it.

I won't go back in the café
so I wander the shutdown strip mall
past all the For Rent signs

till I come to a storefront sign that says
Come In! FREE coffee, handwritten
in faded marker on rippled typing paper.

Inside, the sour smell should send me
packing: stale coffee, stale bodies,
all stained early Van Gogh brown

people huddled into themselves on
cracked vinyl chairs. An overhead bulb
spills light, but grey prevails.

This shelter makes the restaurant an
oasis. "Always carry a dime,"
my mother's distant voice whispers.

I cling to my beige leather purse,
that haunting voice a comfort
and a start.

For an instant I'm one with them,
nameless, no way out.
My knees give and I have

to sit, touching the hard
plastic surface
with my coat.

Logic tugs at the edge of my fright/
flight impulse: I drove the car here,
the doors are locked, so

those keys have to be with me.
My husband often says, How come
you lose your keys so much?

He laughs, tolerant and smug.
I think I might start screaming as
I strive to stay calm, staring

into my bag for my missing keys
to my life
three hours away.

III. SETTLING

Skywriting

I must be shedding:
a chocolate brown bra, my
battery-powered toothbrush,
the book on writing I'd earmarked
for workshop—all in my hands, then
gone.

I've been talking about paring
my possessions, my lifestyle, the
collections of vintage pins and dishes and
books that feel more like rocks
weighing down my fingers than
treasures.

So I retreat to Nimrod where
one room is my haven, one drawer
all the space I use to hold my belongings.
I learn summer after summer
that I don't need much in my life to be
satisfied.

Yet I return home to more debts than dollars,
a closet full of suits I hate to wear,
shoes that hurt my feet, stuff
stacked by my bed that's like an
archeological dig for someone else's
life.

I know the objective correlative
here, the life lesson that's smacked
me in the face for twenty years.
It's the good green witch skywriting
Surrender, Dorothy: Go home
and live your life more simply.
Surrender.

Growing Wild

Wild onions are taking over
my front lawn, an affront
to the former owner who landscaped
with an eye to harmony and control.

A dogwood stick I planted from
the end-of-the-season bin didn't make it;
a few Lenten roses—not really roses at all—
poke through beneath the tree's dead twigs.

An indefatigable Juniper I purchased
in the fall, never planted, yellows
in its too-small pot.
I somehow lack the family gardening skill.

Or is it some yen for order I don't have?
Mother and both her sisters, even Cousin Lynne,
turn green space into showy places, Garden Club
gardens, Aunt Helen's yard like a formal English park.

I look up, wondrous:
pear petals blow like snow across the lawn;
plum tree, camellia, redbud in bloom—
nature's wild glory without the slightest calming touch
from me.

Cast-Offs

Two red glass globes,
candles encased in white plastic webbing,
the shape of a Magic Eight Ball:
they wait for me on a flea market table.
The sticker on the bottom
still says Hills, 97 cents,
in faint blue type.

Amid the dusty discards
these never-used trifles
jolt me, remind me of
my summer backyard,
playing outside in the dark,
our redwood picnic
table under the mimosa,
junebugs in blue Mason jars.

Those childhood summers
we stayed up past dark,
my two brothers and me,
played with our neighbors,
the five Mooneys,
with only dimestore candles
to light our tree fort.

"How much?" I ask the old timer.
"Fifty cents for the pair?" he barters back.
Two quarters outstretched, I lift my memories,
smell the faint citronella,
start to ask *What happened?*

But they're only cast-off
candles, concealing no
magic answers.

Women, Bags

Egg cases deck the shoreline
strung together like a spine, yellowed, tough:
opened, they're full of tiny conch shells
hidden in that placental nest
growing safe, minute knobbed whelks
no larger than fingernail clippings

As a girl, carrying my mama's pocketbook
grown-up, play-acting, pretending to be a mama myself

Full grown, I carry my own
purses, filled with minutiae of a woman's
many lives

That jump-rope rhyme echoes in my ear
like sea sounds from a conch shell:
Along came the doctor, along came the nurse,
along came the lady with the alligator purse

I had an alligator purse with matching pumps
in those days of cotillion and husband hunting
and modeling at the Tea Room while
Eddie Weaver played the organ

Around the same time I owned a
black silk and silver thread embroidered evening bag,
the size of a book, from Miz Pemberton's trip around the world.
Did I send a proper thank-you note?

In college I carried a cherished Greek bag,
dreaming one day of flying to the isles
of Artemis, Athena, the woman-born Hestia
to explore ancient relics, whispers of women
before me

Thrift store shopping with my husband
I found a Goodwill bargain, a vintage Coach
shoulder bag for fifteen dollars
Tres chic

He gave me antique reticules, some silver,
some linked goldish metal, monogrammed,
embroidered, embossed, chained
reminding me of days of high fashion,
the Titanic. Some I use for dress-up.

My purses, my pocketbooks, my bags:
organized, disorganized, changeable;
heavy, light, found, lost;
small, compact, compartmentalized, wide open

When did women first carry purses?
Athena never did, that goddess of power and intellect.
Neither did Harriet Tubman, more like a croaker sack
as she tunneled her way to freedom over and over.
When Sally Ride rode no bag was tucked in her
Astronaut outfit
Surely Kate Chopin never imagined Edna Pontellier
swimming out to the horizon
dragging a purse

Yet I have a history of pocketbooks, bags, reticules, purses
a legacy of toting diaper bags, shopping bags, backpack, briefcase
Even homeless women often lug a bag of some sort,
green, plastic, full of second-, third-hand scraps,
remnants of their lives

Email: Women's March Foundation: "It's in the bag."

A money clip or wallet won't suffice for
women. We grow, protect, define, nurture,
pass on, provide, shelter, escape, move over, move up
move on, transform into the future
embedding our grains of sand, our seeds,
our shell fragments.

Continuity

Ray tail, seagull feathers, foggy beach glass:
seeing these in the strip of ocean's remnants
reminds me
of years wandering
this same stretch of sand.

We shed our skin every seven years.
These grains of sand are each different now,
yet continuity engulfs my feet,
blows damp air through my hair,
holds the horizon in place while everything else
changes.

This spot became mine when, swollen with
my first child, I walked to the shoreline
light as a bubble, skirt lifted by salt air,
welcomed,
placed.

That moment belonged to me to polish,
like silver. Sand, a kind of earth,
grounds me in time and space.
Everything else twists and shifts in ways
I can't control.

I own the memories of bloated
green bananas washed ashore, meteor
showers in August dark, drip castles to occupy
the babies while my mind
wandered.

I walk along this shore, skin shed six times,
my singular self here, seeing again
every ray tail, seagull feather, and translucent piece
of beach glass.

Resurrection Lilies

Every August the resurrection lilies bloom,
the color of a flower girl's blushing cheeks.
Their common name is naked lady; they stretch
in the sunlight, suspended from firm green stalks
unclothed by leafy skirts.

Five ladies go down to swim, naked,
cloaked in early moonlight, skin the color
of bisque dolls. Four float in tubes made light
as lily pads while one bobs around them
suspended in clear water, arms and legs
waving like daylilies in the breeze.

A bat flies sentry to keep away insect
intruders. Stars sparkle within grasp,
singular and beautiful, not crowded like
city sidewalks. A single shooter, only
a brief flash, arcs across the sky's dark ceiling.

Enough, this evening, a bouquet of memories
to press in a locket, to make a garland, a bridal crown
of recollections, each jewel a star, a refracted naked lady,
all part of an ancient river celebration.

Afloat, one woman describes her book of childhood
poems, a naughty black fairy who'd strayed
down a sooty chimney, the ink drawing of the curious
creature at the center of a circle, coddled and bathed by her fair sisters.

These women, encircled in the moonlight, safe,
scattered in the water like random stars overhead,
hear the breeze whisper their names, these questions:
Can you ever see the stars on a moonlit night?
Can naked lady lilies be resurrected each August?

The answers rise clear as the water, clear
as a dragonfly's wings on that cool August night:
Yes, the stars shimmer.
Yes, the bat's wings flap.
Yes, the ladies glistening in the river laugh,
Oh yes.

I grow things

No gardener I, but
I grow things:

a seeding bed of warts on one knee

skin tags buried in my naval

four zygotes clinging to my sturdy woman wall:
morning glories

strings of cysts in my breasts, like
champagne grapes, the
radiologist says

a perfect round pea-sized ball,
milky and gossamer, a small universe unto itself
tucked under my arm, hidden, like a morelle

uterine sacs, a civilization of them,
scraped away like plaque on my teeth
uprooted like dandelions

even a teratoma, with teeth, hair, and
bones—I wish she'd finished growing, too

this latest, thyroid nodules,
could grow into a goiter, that
monstrous human weedpod, enough to
convince a woman she is cursed
or, at the very least, not quite right.
Dr. Green did it, in the hospital room, with
a needle. I, not a clue

my weeds, my seedlings, my volunteers, my children:
my body, my garden

Greek Mythology

Not Buckroe Beach,
not Nags Head,
not Oahu:
Askeli Beach
Poros
Greek waters

Mary Renault
Edith Hamilton
The Odyssey
Dr. Laura Sumner, Greek Art & Archeology prof par excellence

The Athens Taverna
Ordering marides
Saying kalispera

Old couple, her in her bra, every day at 5 at Askeli Beach:
Swimming laps
He towels her off
Did they ever long for more?

Finding Greek coins at a secret trash site
Where fishermen ferry us for American dollars

When did I start looking beyond the playground across the street,
Miz Daughtery in front of the bio lab with her white bun—asking me to be her lab assistant,
the chicken a la gravy my grandmother cooked
to an Agean Beach
a Greek tavern
Kalimera, yogurt and honey
lost treasure

When did that moment of longing shift beyond the boy the next row over,
my need to be Best Personality,
my yearning for a husband to take care of me.

All I saw on Oahu, R&R '68, was the bed in the Ilikai hotel,
Do Ho's restaurant, Do Ho singing Tiny Bubbles under tiki lights,
my brother-and sister-in-law

Where was curiosity, hunger for more, awareness of wider horizons, Greek seas?

I read of poets who always wanted more;
I wanted so little
but didn't know it

Charlotte Gregg Morgan grew up in the "Christ-haunted South" of Richmond, Virginia, caught between strict Baptist dictates and confusion over "massive resistance" to the Civil Rights movement. Sin and guilt and "manners" were a way of life.

Morgan's poems have appeared in *The Hollins Critic, Streetlight, Artemis*, and other literary journals and juried public readings.

Her first novel, *One August Day*, was nominated for the annual fiction award by the Library of Virginia. *Protecting Elvis* is available on Amazon or at Barnes & Noble. Kirkus Review (Oct. 19, 2016) called the novel "A subtle, affecting glimpse into the lives of a trio of singular women molded by the works and personal character of a rock icon." The most recent novel, *The Family*, explores the seductive power of religion for a young woman seeking family and a sense of belonging.

One of Morgan's short stories is included in The Pushcart Prize Collection XXIV. She holds an MFA from Virginia Commonwealth University, where she studied with famed Southern author Lee Smith and "Macarthur Genius" Paule Marshall. Cathryn Hankla has guided her development as a poet.

Morgan's fiction examines the lives of women, their compelling inner conflicts as they face the demanding struggles of complicated external lives, and the difficulty forming and sustaining independence. Poems convey those same themes in her personal life as well as the places that informed her development as a woman and writer. The complexity as well as the majesty of the south as a unique region emerge from Charlotte Morgan's stories and poems.

Morgan is writer-in-residence each summer at Nimrod Hall Summer Arts Program where she works with writers in all stages of their careers. She lives in Lynchburg, Virginia with her artist husband John Dure Morgan and two sassy standard poodles.

www.ingramcontent.com/pod-product-compliance
Lightning Source LLC
LaVergne TN
LVHW041558070426
835507LV00011B/1169